IMAGES
of America

GRIFFISS AIR FORCE BASE

The military legacy of Rome dates all the way back to Fort Stanwix during the Revolutionary War. Rome mayor William Valentine is christening the B-52 *Spirit of Fort Stanwix*. (Rome Historical Society.)

On the cover: A group of F-4 Corsairs line the runway at Griffiss in 1944. Please see page 34. (Rome Historical Society.)

IMAGES
of America

GRIFFISS AIR FORCE BASE

Peter M. Leonard

ARCADIA
PUBLISHING

Published by Arcadia Publishing
Charleston SC, Chicago IL, Portsmouth NH, San Francisco CA

Printed in the United States of America

Library of Congress Catalog Card Number: 2007943796

For all general information contact Arcadia Publishing at:
Telephone 843-853-2070
Fax 843-853-0044
E-mail sales@arcadiapublishing.com
For customer service and orders:
Toll-Free 1-888-313-2665

Visit us on the Internet at www.arcadiapublishing.com

Soldiers of the 100th Aviation Squadron receive prizes after participating in a boxing competition held at Madison Square Garden in 1943. (Kevin Kelley.)

CONTENTS

ACKNOWLEDGMENTS

First and foremost, I thank all the men and women who were stationed or worked at Griffiss Air Force Base, for without you there would be no book.

I am thankful to the Rome Historical Society for allowing me the use of many pictures from its Griffiss archives. It is further credited as RHS in the following pages. And a special thank-you to Robert Avery, Ann Swanson, and Michael Huchko for helping me in this process.

Kevin Kelley, a fellow Griffiss historian, provided me with several of the unique and candid World War II–period photographs in this book. Kevin's knowledge of base history was a real asset to my project.

I would also like to thank Margo Studios of Rome for allowing me to use several postcard images taken by photographer Anthony Mario. Thank you to Rebekah Collinsworth of Arcadia for her help and guidance. Thank you to my mom, Johanna Leonard, and my sister, Debbie Leonard, for helping with all the little projects in assembling this work. And to my dad, Peter Leonard, who passed away in 2003 and also shared in my interest of local history and was a former air policeman with the 4039th Strategic Wing from 1959 to 1963.

INTRODUCTION

Located in the heart of New York State is the city of Rome. Rome can easily be termed as a military town. With two major waterways converging into what the Oneida Indians referred to as the De-O-Wain-Sta, or the Great Carrying Place, it was possible to travel from Canada to the Atlantic Ocean using these ancient waterways. Realizing the importance of such a geological feature, the British in 1758 constructed a very large fort that was named in honor of the general who oversaw the construction, John Stanwix.

Fort Stanwix did not see any action in the French and Indian War. By the time 1775 rolled around the British had abandoned the fort, which the Continental army then took control of. Col. Peter Gansevoort and the 3rd New York Regiment, 700 strong, repaired and readied the fort for battle. On August 3, 1777, an army of loyalists, loyalist Native Americans, and British regulars demanded Gansevoort surrender the fort. Gansevoort refused, and a siege was laid against the defenders. In a brave show of defiance, the first Stars and Stripes were unfurled in battle in front of the enemy.

Word of the siege reached Gen. Nicholas Herkimer, who was the commander of the Tryon County Militia. He immediately mobilized his men and began to march to the fort to aid the defenders. Six miles from the fort on the hills of Oriskany, Herkimer and his men were ambushed by British regulars and loyalist Native Americans. The fight was abandoned after several hours of fierce bloody combat and a raging thunderstorm. Both sides suffered high casualties; General Herkimer was among them.

In all, the siege lasted 21 days before the British fell back to Canada, a costly mistake that would eventually cost them the state of New York in the Revolution. Following the war a state arsenal was built near the Mohawk River. A federal arsenal was then constructed on Dominick Street, of which the commandant's house still stands today. In 1817, it was here that the first shovel of dirt was overturned to begin construction on the Erie Canal. Romans fought in every major war and conflict from the Revolution onward, forging an impressive honor roll, with the patriotism of Fort Stanwix behind all their actions.

The turbulent affairs of the world in 1939 set the war department about planning for another global war. It was just a matter of when the United States would again be drawn into another global conflict, therefore preparations were necessary. In 1940, Rome appeared on a list as a possible site for the construction of a new air depot. City politicians wasted no time in courting the war department to select Rome in its search. After tests taken showed that Rome in fact was an ideal location for the base, it was then approved by Congress.

Construction began in the summer of 1941, and after the attack on Pearl Harbor in December, completion of the base in record time was made a top priority of the war department. The primary function of the Rome Air Depot was that of storage and aircraft maintenance. It became home to the 100th Aviation Squadron, an all African American unit, and also a station for many Women's Army Auxiliary Corps (WAAC) members.

Following the war, the base was renamed to Griffiss and the mission of the base was expanded to include communications research and development. An air defense mission guarded the skies of the eastern seaboard. Fighter planes of the 465th and 27th Fighter Interceptor Squadrons patrolled the Eastern Air Defense Sector on a daily basis. Rome Air Development Center relayed the first successful satellite communications in 1960.

The 1960s brought in the Strategic Air Command (SAC) and the B-52 stratobombers for global security. Several units of the base were deployed to Vietnam in support of military operations and then again in Operation Desert Storm. Griffiss B-52s were the first in the U.S. Air Force to be armed with air launched cruise missiles (ALCMs).

Sadly, following Desert Storm, several bases appeared on the Base Realignment and Closure Committee (BRACC) list of installations to be closed; Griffiss was among them. Regardless of the endless list of awards, accomplishments, and innovations that came out of Griffiss, it was not enough to save the base. The citizenry of Rome rallied and put up a worthy fight, but in the end the last B-52 took off in 1995, and Griffiss Air Force Base is now a part of military history. In 1999, the former Griffiss Air Force Base was used as the location of the 30th anniversary of Woodstock.

One

AIR DEPOT
COMES TO TOWN

Man has always had a dream of flying, and in the early 20th century that dream became a reality. During the early years of aviation, major installations were not required to accommodate aircraft. The plane shown above landed at the old Teugega Country Club in Rome during 1920.

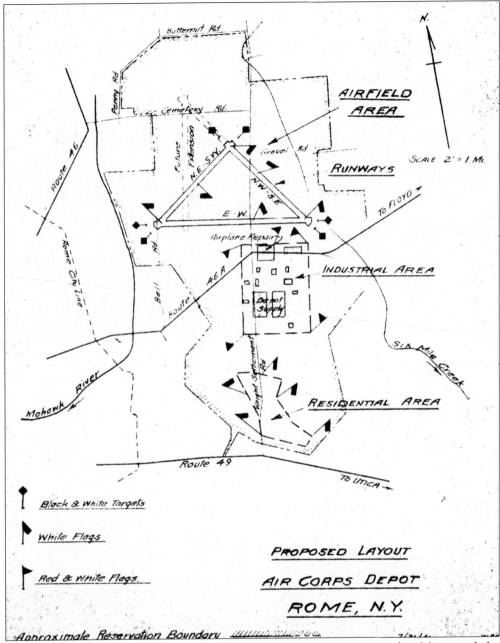

Capitalizing on the strategic location of Rome near major waterways and rail lines and the willingness of the City of Rome to cooperate with the military, a group of engineers was dispatched to do preliminary tests to see if a base in Rome would be beneficial. With the tests producing positive results, the war department approved the project and the Rome Air Depot was activated on June 28, 1941. Capt. Kenneth Nichols was appointed to oversee the $14 million construction project. Farmlands outside the city limits were acquired in what was called the Wright Settlement area. The Rome Air Depot was expected to employ 3,000 workers.

Bidding for the construction project was intense, but in the end two companies were awarded the war department contract, Turner Construction Company of New York City and Louis Mayersohn of Albany. Ground was officially broken on August 2, 1941, and construction began immediately. Above, ground is being prepared to make room for the supply and quartermaster areas. Below, workers are setting up concrete forms to construct the east-west runway near the Wright Settlement Road. It would be one of three runways at the depot.

The depot was to have two major missions, supply and aircraft maintenance and repair. Two major supply building warehouses were to be completed. A unique feature was the addition of rail lines that would bring the goods right to the supply buildings for easy loading and unloading.

Piles are being driven to form the foundation of the engine test building. Military planes located on the northeastern seaboard in need of routine maintenance or in need of engine repair or rebuilding would receive that service at Rome.

Work progressed through the bad weather on the runways. In total, the Rome Air Depot would have three runways in a triangular layout. Shown above is a wide variety of construction machinery belonging to the Louis Mayersohn Company.

Several airplane hangars are being built to store the aircraft and to do year-round repairs when the weather in Rome is not so nice outside. Work progresses on Hangar 3 as the framework is completed.

When Pearl Harbor was attacked on December 7, 1941, the completion of the Rome Air Depot was made a top priority by the war department. Construction continued through the harsh Upstate New York winter. Slowly the engine repair building is starting to take shape. Below, Depot Supply Building 1 is shown from the interior; note the railcars bringing in building supplies.

Finishing touches are being added to the quartermaster garage building. This building was used to house trucks and equipment needed for facilities and ground maintenance to keep the appearance of the depot up to military standards.

The Rome Air Depot as seen from the air, in accordance with a war department goal, was completed in record time. Depot Supply Buildings 1 and 2 can be seen in the center of the picture. Behind that are the four airplane hangars, and the runways appear in the distance. Off to the left can be seen the headquarters building. (RHS.)

In the interim, while the depot was being constructed, the army began a troop buildup. The Rome Air Depot was placed under the command of the Air Service Command. Since there were no quarters available at the time, the majority of them were housed at the Syracuse Fairgrounds.

Construction at the depot was completed by November 1942. However, the runway had been open since February. An A-17 was the first plane to land at the new depot on February 18. Troops being quartered at Syracuse were now moved to Rome. (RHS.)

At 8:00 a.m. on November 7, 1942, the first American flag was raised over the depot in the presence of all the officers who were now present for duty. Col. George McPike became the first commander at the Rome Air Depot. He officially moved his temporary headquarters from the Jenny House to the new headquarters building at the depot. Colonel McPike, a World War I veteran, was called back to active duty and served as depot commander for a year before being transferred to a base in China. (Above, RHS; below, Kevin Kelley.)

During World War II, the army was still segregated in the fact that African American men were put into special units commanded by Caucasian officers. The 100th Aviation Squadron was one of those units and was activated at the depot on September 8, 1942. (Kevin Kelley.)

A soldier identified as Cpl. John Hilton, shown in the center, was just awarded the Soldier's Medal by depot commander Col. Clarence Kane. The Soldier's Medal is awarded to soldiers who distinguish themselves with an act of noncombat heroism, and it usually involves some act of lifesaving. (RHS.)

Many men of the 100th were experienced boxers before the war. In 1943, the *New York Daily News* hosted an All Soldiers Golden Gloves competition at Madison Square Garden in New York City. Rome was represented by five boxers, all of whom were working at the depot: Douglas Ratford, Harrison Leonard, Thomas Branch, Cicero Davis, and Mell Jordan. The 100th Aviation put up a good fight, and although they did not win the competition they all did place high in the standings. (Kevin Kelley.)

Pistol Packin' Mama

Another military milestone during World War II was the introduction of the Women's Army Auxiliary Corps (WAAC) later known as WAC. Prior to this women were not allowed to carry out any official military duties, with the exception of nursing. Although they were not allowed to serve in combat zones, they did take on many of the same job functions as their male counterparts at stateside bases to free the males up for combat zone duty. Gen. Douglas MacArthur called the WACs his best soldiers because they worked harder, complained less, and were better disciplined than male soldiers. Below are some of the Rome Air Depot WACs marching in a parade through downtown Rome. (Kevin Kelley.)

The paperwork required to run the Rome Air Depot was immense. During the peak years of 1944 and 1945, there were over 19,000 employees at the base and the majority were civilians. Both military and civilian workers processed the mountains of paperwork running the gambit from payroll to supply requisitions. The supply areas were processing and shipping in excess of 100,000 items a month. The workweek consisted of a period of 48 hours to support the war effort. (RHS.)

UNITED FOR VICTORY

"KEEP 'EM FLYING"

Often referred to as the home front movement, large numbers of women entered the workforce to support the soldiers, sailors, and marines. Popular slogans of the time drove the point home, like "Remember Pearl Harbor" and, in particular at Rome, "Keep 'em Flying."

Rosie the Riveter was a generic term used for women doing mechanical or industrial work. Shown here are two lady airplane mechanics working on the repair of a B-17 engine at the Rome Air Depot. (RHS.)

Airplanes were flown to Rome from all theaters of war for repair. A quota was set and met that 1,000 engines needed to be overhauled or repaired each month in direct support of the war mission. (RHS.)

More often than not, enemy fire was intense and produced severe damage to the aircraft. If able to make the voyage back to Rome, the aircraft would then be refurbished and repaired. After a few successful test flights the aircraft would be returned to active duty. (RHS.)

The military workers at the base developed a hearty appetite after a long day of work at the depot. The dining hall is lavishly decorated in preparation for the upcoming Thanksgiving dinner. (RHS.)

It was not uncommon to have over 250 inches of snow fall during a winter season in Rome, not to mention the extremely cold weather that accompanied the snow. Crews worked around the clock clearing the roads and runways so they could "Keep 'em Flying." This crew stopped for a minute to pose for the camera in 1945.

Propaganda is a very useful tool during times of war. This giant concrete statue was erected at the depot. It was meant to inspire those who saw it by the symbolic words on its base, "So it's a fight you want, huh!" referencing the sneak attack at Pearl Harbor. For those who could not serve due to age or health reasons, an opportunity was created for them to help through the war bond campaign rallies. Millions of dollars were raised to support the war effort. (RHS.)

Baseball was the great American pastime; however, during the war years many leagues suspended games due to the lack of male athletes. Again the ladies of America and the Rome Air Depot stepped up to the plate to provide that service. The Rome Air Depot league drew large crowds of spectators and was a popular way to spend weekends after a long week of work. (Kevin Kelley.)

Smoking was not allowed in the engine repair or storage areas due to the flammability of the fuel. WAC Mabel Duncan, nicknamed Dunk, is seen here having her butt put out in a proper receptacle. (Kevin Kelley.)

Sometimes nothing beats spending some quiet time reading a book, especially after a hard day of work. Several WACs are shown here in the reading room at one of the dormitories. The depot did have a well-stocked library with over 3,800 books. (Kevin Kelley.)

The 350-seat base chapel was dedicated on November 8, 1942. Events of the day included a baptism and a wedding. Masses were only offered in Catholic and Protestant faiths at the depot. The first chaplain described it as "a soul hospital where those broken down in heart or with sin may be healed." (Margo Studio.)

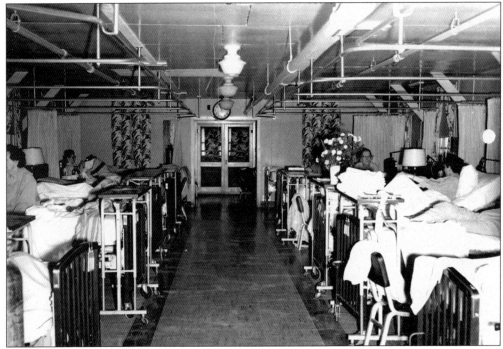

The original depot hospital was an assortment of 22 buildings all connected with covered walkways and hallways. As with any civilian hospital, it was fully staffed and provided the same level of care to the patients, although as seen, privacy was not an issue. (RHS.)

Although the baby boomer age followed World War II, the population of the base increased daily with the births of several babies. The hospital did boast a modern maternity ward and child care services for the mothers. The baby shown in the picture is Robert Wisner Jr., who was born at the Rome Air Depot Hospital. The picture was appropriately titled "Picture of the year!" (Right, Kevin Kelley; below, RHS.)

The flight test building was also the home to the flight tower, which controlled all incoming and outgoing flights into the depot. It provided a 360-degree bird's-eye view of the depot. (RHS.)

The sturdy bunker-style buildings on the flight line housed the engine test center. By war's end over 15,000 people were trained as airplane mechanics at the depot and 14,000 aircraft engines were being stored at the depot. (RHS.)

Planes are lined up end over end inside of Hangar 100 awaiting repair at the depot. During the time period, the Rome Air Depot opened until the end of the war in 1945, thousands of aircraft were sent for repairs. (RHS.)

The Rome Air Depot Fire Department is shown responding to an emergency landing of a B-29 Superfortress. Fortunately, there was no major damage to the aircraft or crew flying it to the depot for repair. (RHS.)

Two women on the runway are directing traffic among an assortment of aircraft at the depot. Pictured are the AT-9 and BT-13, both used to train pilots. The tail section of a C-47 can also be seen. (RHS.)

The crew of a B-29 bomber is preparing to start the engines. Although the B-29 was a very reliable bomber, it suffered from constant and sometimes catastrophic engine problems in combat conditions until a series of modifications corrected those troubles. (RHS.)

The B-17 Flying Fortress was the workhorse of the bomber fleet, with more than 12,000 produced during the war. The B-17 was a very reliable aircraft and was well armed with several machine gun turrets. A row of B-17s can be seen along the ramp at the depot. (RHS.)

Nose art was a way of personalizing the aircraft, and often the design had a special significance to the crew. This B-17 was not as famous as the *Memphis Belle*, but it did see some serious combat in Japan. It ended up in Rome after being hit six times by a Japanese 20-millimeter cannon during a night raid that resulted in two crew members being wounded. (RHS.)

The Republic P-47 Thunderbolt sits on the ramp at the Rome Air Depot. The P-47 was armed with eight machine guns, and its ability to achieve high speeds made this airplane one of the finest combat fighters in World War II. (Kevin Kelley.)

In anticipation of a potential hurricane along the Virginia coast, 184 aircraft were relocated to the depot to avoid the storm. The F-4 Corsair was among them and can be seen lining the ramp. The F-4 was primarily used by the navy and saw heavy combat in the Pacific theater. (RHS.)

The B-25 Mitchell delivered the first bombs on Japan since the surprise on Pearl Harbor. The B-25 saw action in both theaters of the war. This one is awaiting takeoff at the depot. (Kevin Kelley.)

One airplane capable of striking fear into the enemy during the war was the B-29 Superfortress. B-29s delivered the first atomic bomb attacks bringing the war to an end in Japan. This is the same aircraft pictured on page 31 after being repaired.

ROME AIR TECHNICAL SERVICE COMMAND

Welcomes You

This Is Your Depot

The Maintenance Division display and tour will be open from 1:00 P.M. to 4:45 P.M. All are invited to see the Machine Shops and facilities of this depot.

Several different types of aircraft will be landing, taking-off and flying around the field during the course of the afternoon. Two way radio conversation between the control tower and these aircraft may be heard over the loudspeaker system.

SPECIAL EVENTS ON OTHER SIDE

SMOKING IS NOT PERMITTED IN ANY OF THE BUILDINGS

Families and friends heard story after story of battlefield exploits. Even Hollywood was turning out movie after movie with a war-based theme. When the depot hosted an open house it was no surprise that over 130,000 people showed up. Many were curious to see first hand the machines and technology they read about in the newspapers and letters or saw in the movies. To entice the crowds, many displays were set up and aircraft were set up to allow visitors to look inside. (RHS.)

Crowds are beginning to huddle around the famed B-17. Also in the same area of display is a P-38 fighter airplane and a C-47 cargo aircraft. The engine test building can be seen in the rear. (RHS.)

A T-6 trainer aircraft is completely dwarfed by the immense size of the B-29 Superfortress. For size comparison, the T-6 is only as long as the wingtip on the B-29. (RHS.)

Many troops and wounded soldiers were transported in the C-47 Skytrain aircraft. Actually the C-47 was the military version of the Douglas DC-3 used by commercial airlines. A P-38 appears in the background. (RHS.)

The B-17 exhibit was so popular that a special platform was constructed to allow two rows of visitors to get a close look at the famed bomber. (RHS.)

A bomber equivalent in firepower and payload to the B-17 was the B-24 Liberator. However, it was not favored by the combat troops, but it was also the most produced aircraft during the war. (RHS.)

This young man is getting an up-close and personal look at the twin machine guns mounted in the nose of an aircraft. Also on the nose are the names and salutations painted by the crew. (RHS.)

Another popular display was the ordnance carried by the bombers. They look small in pictures until one is standing next to one for comparison. Note the soldier smoking near one of the gravity-dropped bombs. (RHS.)

After the war, daily activities were scaled back and the base became a station to separate soldiers from military service. By January 1946 they successfully discharged over 13,000 people from military service. Thousands of local civilian employees were also released from service as the depot resumed its nonwar mission of storage and maintenance. (Kevin Kelley.)

Lt. Col. Townsend Griffiss, a Buffalo, New York, native, was the first American aviator to be killed in World War II, while returning from a training mission in Russia. Located in the heart of Bushy Park in England was Camp Griffiss, named in his honor. This was also the home of Gen. Dwight Eisenhower's SHAEF and it was here that the plans were devised for the invasion of Normandy, France, known forever as D-day. (RHS.)

The year 1947 brought about the separation of the army and the formation of the air force as a separate branch of military service. Likewise, all army air depots would have their designations changed to air force base. In January 1948, the Fort Worth Air Base (Texas) name changed to Griffiss Air Force Base. Legend has it that the signage and paperwork for Griffiss was mistakenly sent to the Rome Air Force Base, which was actually supposed to be named Carswell Air Force Base. On September 20, 1948, that is how Rome became the home of Griffiss Air Force Base.

Two

AIR DEFENSE COMMAND

A visitor poses in front of the nose of an F-86 aircraft. F-86s were flown by the 27th Fighter Interceptor Squadron (27th FIS). The F-86 Sabrejet was a widely used aircraft and entered service in the late 1940s. It was armed with a .50-caliber machine gun and could be modified to carry rockets. The F-86 had a range of 1,500 miles and could travel at speeds up to 680 miles per hour. (Margo Studios.)

In 1950, Griffiss was chosen to receive an Air Defense Command mission to defend the skies of the eastern seaboard. To answer that call was the 27th FIS Black Falcons and F-86 jet aircraft. Those would later be replaced with F-89s, F-94s, and finally the F-102 while assigned at Griffiss. It is the oldest fighter squadron in the air force with roots dating all the way back to World War I. Below, a group of 27th pilots stand in front of several F-102s. (RHS.)

During the transition of the F-89 aircraft to Griffiss in 1954, the 27th was upgraded to receive the F-94C Starfire. The F-94 was a two-seat all-weather fighter interceptor that could travel at 600 miles per hour. It was armed with four machine guns, and each wing had a pod holding 24 folding-fin aerial rockets. The close-up view above shows the distinctive yellow and black checker pattern and yellow and black star design on the wing pods. The photograph below shows a row of F-94s on the flight line. (Above, Margo Studios; below, RHS.)

The F-102 Delta Dart or Deuce replaced the fleet of F-94s being flown by the 27th. It was the first in a new series of supersonic fighter interceptor aircraft. Its unique dart-shaped design allowed it to reach speeds of Mach 1.25. Armaments included rockets or Falcon missiles. (Margo Studios.)

For nine years the 27th patrolled the skies above and around Griffiss. The 27th rotated out of Griffiss in October 1959 and moved to Loring Air Force Base in Maine where it continued flying in an air defense capacity. (RHS.)

Following the activation of the 465th FIS in October 1955, the first F-89D jets landed at Griffiss on February 13, 1956, and were immediately put into service. The new all-weather fighters required a crew of two. It had a maximum speed of 630 miles per hour and a range of 1,300 miles. The F-89 was equipped with two wing pods each holding 52 folding-fin aerial rockets known as "Mickey Mouse" to the munitions crews, and the F-89 was also capable of carrying Falcon or Genie (nuclear) rockets.

Col. Frank Keller and Lt. Michael Zaretsky pose in the cockpit of an F-89 after taking the honor of first place in the 1958 William Tell Fighter Championship at Tyndall Air Force Base in Florida. Colonel Keller won after scoring a kill in a special shoot-off match for first place.

The 465th received a hero's welcome upon its return to Griffiss. Colonel Keller is greeted by other pilots of the 465th. In the background the World War II–era statue has been painted with a patch of the 465th to honor its victory at William Tell.

Pilots of the 465th pose with members of the 606th Consolidated Air Maintenance Squadron who were entrusted with the goal of keeping the 465th flying; they are wearing white overalls. They were also present at the 1958 William Tell Championship.

F-89s of the 465th had the unit logo applied to the tail of the aircraft. Yet another distinctive marking of the 465th aircraft are the lightning bolts on the wing pods.

The 465th Fighter Interceptor Squadron was absorbed into the 49th Fighter Interceptor Squadron in 1959, replacing the 27th FIS. The 49th took possession of the new F-101B Voodoo all-weather fighter jet on August 25, 1959, shortly after its activation at Griffiss. The 49th traced its history back to World War II, where it saw heavy combat in the Mediterranean and European theaters of war. (Below, RHS.)

Nicknamed Voodoo because it was considered an ugly airplane by design, it was one of a new series of revolutionary fighters to enter service. This two-seat aircraft was able to achieve a remarkable speed of Mach 1.7 and had a range of 1,500 miles without being aerial refueled. Armaments included four cannons and a payload of four AIM-4 Falcon missiles or two AIM-4 missiles and two Genie nuclear missiles. (Margo Studios.)

The F-106 Delta Dart or Six, as the pilots would refer to it, was a vast improvement over the F-102 Dart. The F-106 was the last of the interceptor models and became the ultimate interceptor for the Tactical Air Command. It could travel at an impressive speed of Mach 2.3 and had a range of 1,800 miles. The F-106 was armed with a 20-millimeter cannon and could carry a payload consisting of four AIM-4 Falcon missiles and either two Falcon nuclear-tipped missiles or a 1.5-kiloton warhead AIR-2 Genie nuclear missile.

Pilots learning to fly while assigned to the 49th received that experience in the T-33 trainer jet. It was normal for newly assigned pilots to practice in the T-33 for a year or two to gain experience before moving on to the Six. The T-33 T-Bird was a highly versatile jet aircraft that required a crew of two to pilot. It could achieve speeds of 600 miles per hour. It could hold a payload of 200 pounds of ordnance and could defend itself in combat with two .50-caliber machine guns.

Griffiss F-106 fighter aircraft went nuclear when it took delivery of the AIR-2 Genie rocket. The Genie was an unguided air-to-air rocket, and it carried a 1.5-kiloton nuclear warhead. The purpose of the Genie was to fire it into a formation of enemy aircraft, and the resulting airborne nuclear explosion would take out those aircraft. Only one live nuclear Genie was ever fired and detonated, and that was during a test in 1957.

Fighter squadrons from Griffiss were no stranger to the William Tell Championship matches held at Tyndall Air Force Base. The 49th was one of the most efficient and highly trained squadron flying the F-106, with many of the pilots logging thousands of flight hours in the same aircraft. This valuable experience was an asset during the competition, especially in 1978 when they took home first place. Even when not in first place, they usually dominated the F-106 category. (Margo Studios.)

The highest honor a fighter squadron could ever achieve was the Hughes Trophy for Excellence in Air Defense. The trophy is awarded by air force headquarters to a fighter squadron based on their air defense effectiveness, skill as an interceptor squadron, safety, maintenance, and readiness to respond. In monetary terms of 1978, the trophy was appraised at $70,000. (RHS.)

Lt. Col. Jim Lowe, center, commander of the 49th, receives the Hughes Trophy on behalf of the squadron at an award ceremony in 1978. The award of the trophy rounded out a good year for the 49th at Griffiss. (RHS.)

F-106s of the 49th fly in formation over the base at a ceremony welcoming them home after receiving the Hughes Trophy in 1978. In the 1980s, the air force started to phase out the interceptor squadrons and the F-106s. Despite its excellent record, the 49th was not spared from closure. In 1987, when the unit was deactivated, it was the last active unit flying the F-106 and boasted some of the most skilled pilots and ground crews in the air force. From here the mission of the fighter interceptor squadrons became a part of air force history. (RHS.)

Although it has seen many name changes throughout the years, the aerial defense of the eastern seaboard lies with the Northeast Air Defense Sector (NEADS). Starting in 1956 as the New York Air Defense Sector, it was the first to become operational with the Semi-Automatic Ground Environment (SAGE) defense system. In the event of an enemy intrusion into eastern airspace, NEADS would then scramble available fighter squadrons to intercept. One notable time occurred in 1962 during the Cuban Missile Crisis when the 49th was scrambled to intercept an alert at Niagara Falls. Most recently during the tragedy of September 11, 2001, NEADS quickly took control of skies minutes after the attacks began, which led to all commercial aircraft being grounded to free up the airspace for military aircraft. (RHS.)

Three

STRATEGIC AIR COMMAND TAKES OVER

The strategic location of Griffiss was known for years, and as the need for global defense expanded, Griffiss also benefited from that expansion. The Strategic Air Command (SAC) was entrusted with preserving the safety of the United States by maintaining an airborne alert force of bomber aircraft all armed with nuclear weapons and a land-based array of intercontinental ballistic missiles. The motto of the SAC was "Peace is our profession."

In 1956, it was decided that the base should be readied for an eventual SAC mission. The runway was to be expanded to a length of two and a quarter miles, and several of the old World War II vintage wooden structures were razed and replaced with modern facilities.

Originally the SAC operated as a tenant unit at Griffiss. Bomber and support missions were dwarfed in comparison to the research and development missions at Griffiss. In 1970, the decision was made that the SAC should take over operational command of Griffiss and all subordinate functions should also fall under their command. (RHS.)

As a result of the new runway and major upgrades to base facilities, the SAC announced in January 1958 that it would assign 1,500 officers and enlisted men to Griffiss. Later that year in August, the 4039th Strategic Wing was activated to carry out that mission. The 4039th was to have assigned to it 15 B-52s and 20 KC-135s. In addition to the flying mission, the 4039th had several subordinate units specializing in weapons, avionics, maintenance, and security. (RHS.)

The B-52 is considered the finest military aircraft ever built by the Boeing Corporation. The first B-52s entered service in 1955 and immediately became the workhorse of the SAC. The B-52 Stratofortress is a long-range strategic bomber capable of delivering massive payloads of conventional bombs or nuclear weapons. It has an impressive wing span of 185 feet and is powered by eight engines. Without refueling it, a crew of six could travel distances up to 4,400 miles. The first B-52 to land at Griffiss was tail number 225, named the *Mohawk Valley*. (Above, RHS; below, Margo Studios.)

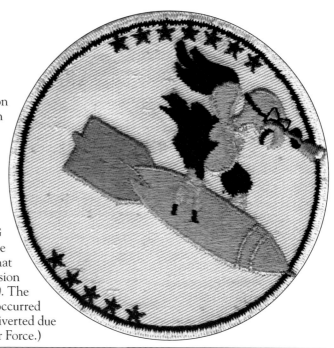

The 75th Bombardment Squadron was assigned to Griffiss in October 1959 as the only flying mission of the 4039th Strategic Wing. A total of 59 officers and 79 airmen transferred from Loring Air Force Base in Maine to staff the new squadron at Griffiss. The 75th would eventually take delivery of 15 G model B-52s. Shown below is the crew of the *Mohawk Valley* that flew the first official B-52 mission into Griffiss on January 12, 1960. The first B-52 to land at Griffiss had occurred a month earlier when one was diverted due to bad weather. (Below, U.S. Air Force.)

KC-135s were a necessity for SAC. Without these aerial tankers the mission of the SAC would have been a failure. The 41st Air Refueling Squadron (AREFS) was activated and assigned to Griffiss to support the 75th Bombardment Squadron B-52s. The first KC-135s actually arrived at Griffiss before the B-52s. *The City of Rome* landed on April 17, 1959. The KC-135 is capable of carrying 83,000 pounds of jet fuel, which it provides to a waiting aircraft through an extension called a boom. (RHS.)

In an effort to immortalize the famous flying units of World War II, the SAC began to rename active duty units. The 4039th Strategic Wing on February 1, 1963, was renamed the 416th Bombardment Wing. In 1970, the SAC assumed the host mission of the base through the 416th. All subordinate units reported directly to the 416th Bombardment Wing. Shown below is the headquarters building of the 416th and office of the base commander. (RHS.)

Since the 75th Bombardment Squadron was not assigned to the 416th, it also was renamed to the 668th Bombardment Squadron. The B-52 was a vast improvement over the A-20 and A-26s it flew during the war. The 668th flew 285 combat missions over France and Germany during World War II, inflicting heavy damage to enemy targets. It earned a Distinguished Unit Citation and a commendation from Gen. George S. Patton for accuracy in destroying targets.

The 416th Combat Defense Squadron, later to be named Security Police Squadron, was the law enforcement and protection arm of the 416th Bombardment Wing. Air policemen could be found everywhere on base from the entrance gates to the flight line where they guarded the aircraft year-round 24 hours a day.

Maj. John Rogers and Provost Marshal James Eggleston receive the newly designed air police shield to be worn on their uniforms from 416th commander Col. Edward Stoddard in 1960. The badge replaced an armband that was previously worn by the air police.

Airman 2nd Class Peter Leonard, a Perth Amboy, New Jersey, native, was one of the first air policemen to be assigned to the 4039th Combat Defense Squadron in 1959. Griffiss was on high alert during the tense standoff during the Cuban Missile Crisis in October 1962. Base photographer Frank Ponessa positioned himself on the ground using Leonard's legs to frame this photograph of him guarding a KC-135. This photograph, titled "SAC Sentry Stands Guard," went on to win many awards in the Eighth Air Force, including SAC Photo of the Month.

Under the SAC, alerts and practice drills were a common occurrence with names like Operation Chrome Dome. The cold war necessitated keeping a squadron of B-52s and KC-135s airborne at all times so in the event of a sneak attack, at least one squadron would be able to deliver a counterstrike with nuclear capabilities. Alerts took place at all times of the day and night to keep the SAC ever ready to meet any threat. (RHS.)

Special facilities were built for the crews and families that were on alert. There were long tunnels that opened onto the alert aprons where the aircraft were located. While waiting, airmen passed the time as they wanted. (RHS.)

It cannot be stressed enough that the SAC mission was achieved through training, discipline, and readiness to respond within seconds notice. Day or night, a sneak attack could come, and the SAC made sure there was a large enough force of dedicated men and women to carry out that enormous mission with dedication, precision, and accuracy. (RHS.)

Rain, sleet, snow, and extreme heat did not stop the many ground, maintenance, and munitions crews from carrying out the duties required to keep the B-52s and KC-135s ready for battle. Many Griffiss veterans will attest to the extremely cold temperatures that could be found out on the flight line during the famous Upstate New York winters. (RHS.)

It was only a matter of time until hostilities in Southeast Asia drew the United States into the conflict. B-52s from Griffiss were rotated in and out of the war zone regularly starting in 1968 to support the Arc Light B-52 strategic bombing campaign against North Vietnamese targets. Fortunately, no B-52s from Griffiss were lost or damaged during the war. (RHS.)

"The Miracle Take-off," as this photograph has come to be known, shows the tremendous skills pilots displayed with split-second decisions. This B-52 upon takeoff was almost lost by banking too far to the right, but quick action by the crew allowed it to recover the aircraft and get it airborne.

Probably the single hardest duty of any airman was to say goodbye to family and friends before departing for war. A crew member of the 41st AREFS is expressing those feelings prior to departing for Southeast Asia. (RHS.)

December 15, 1964, saw the first wave of 41st AREFS KC-135s being deployed to Vietnam to provide air refueling during Operation Foreign Legion. The larger of the tanker missions came in 1968 and was known as Operation Young Tiger. Millions of pounds of fuel were boomed through thousands of hours of flight time. The last Young Tiger mission took place on October 6, 1975. (RHS.)

The B-52 in itself was a versatile weapon. In addition to a vast array of electronic countermeasures, each B-52 was installed with a tail section armed with guns. The tail gunner was the only enlisted man on the crew of a B-52. The payload that was carried could be diverse, but during Vietnam gravity-dropped bombs were common. The wings could also hold an assortment of munitions, but the Griffiss B-52s were armed with AGM-28 Hound Dog missiles. The tail gunner position was eliminated in 1991, and the guns were removed from the B-52. (RHS.)

It is impossible to list all the competitions, commendations, awards, and trophies that were won by the 416th Bombardment Wing in this book. Some of the more prestigious honors include the General John Ryan Trophy for the best B-52 unit in bombing, best wing in the Combat Weapons Loading Competition, Eighth Air Force Golden Bomber Award, SAC Hall of Fame Certificate, and SAC Bombing and Navigation Competitions. (RHS.)

Departing for a major competition was always a cause for celebration in the Rome community. This B-52 was renamed the *Pride of the Mohawk Valley*. Shown at the far left is Rome mayor William Valentine and next to him Oneida County executive Charles Lanigan, who christened the B-52 moments earlier. (RHS.)

The crew of the *Pride of the Mohawk Valley*, Robert Johnson, Robert Kirtley, George Dolan, Henry Shinol, Thomas O'Brien, and William Clouse, is seen before departing for the 1965 SAC Bombing and Navigation Competition at Fairchild Air Force Base. (RHS.)

The most fitting honor for the Revolutionary War defenders of Fort Stanwix to receive was B-52 tail number 250 being renamed in their honor. Mayor Valentine polishes a part of the logo, which shows the outline of Fort Stanwix and the first American flag raised in battle. (RHS.)

The crew of the *Spirit of Fort Stanwix* is making some last-minute plans and plotting strategies to use at the 1966 SAC Bombing and Navigation Competition before departing Griffiss. (RHS.)

The most top secret airplane in the air force was the SR-71 Blackbird. Its missions were held at the highest levels of security, and many probably do not know of its mission at Griffiss. During the 1973 Yom Kippur War in Israel, Griffiss was used as an operating location for the Blackbird reconnaissance missions. This very rare photograph shows tail number 764 before a mission.

Two years later in 1975, tail number 955 landed at Griffiss. There are several conflicting stories as to what the mission was, but no confirmable answer has ever appeared other than it was at Griffiss in 1975.

To test the effectiveness of SAC, Global Shield 1979 was ordered by the commander of the SAC. This was the largest SAC alert exercise in 20 years. A convoy of supply trucks is lined up along the flight line ready to assist in Global Shield. (RHS.)

A KC-135, tail number 3549, takes off following the activation of the Global Shield alert. Every SAC base around the world participated in this exercise.

The 416th was given the honor of being the first B-52 wing to receive the new Boeing AGM-86 air-launched cruise missiles. The first two arrived on December 16, 1982. The B-52s underwent special modifications to allow them to carry up to 20 missiles. The warhead could be nuclear or a conventional explosive. The latest in technology and design, the cruise missile would later be proven to be very effective in Operation Desert Storm. Vice Pres. George Bush gets to view one at the Rome Air Development Center's test chamber in 1983. (RHS.)

Following the August 1990 invasion of Kuwait by Iraq, over 1,300 Griffiss personnel were deployed to over 26 locations during the height of Operation Desert Storm. Provisional bomb wings were set up in the United Kingdom and the 1702nd Air Refueling Wing (Provisional) set up its base of operations at Camp Nacirema in Seeb, Oman. The name Nacirema is actually American spelled backward and was the result of a contest held to name the base. KC-135s of the 1702nd AREFW(P) flew over 1,100 sorties and passed over 100 million pounds of jet fuel during Operation Desert Storm; among them was the 41st AREFS. (U.S. Air Force.)

Twelve Griffiss B-52s were deployed to three locations during the conflict. The 801st Provisional Bomb Wing was based at Moron Air Force Base, Spain; the 806th at RAF Fairford, United Kingdom; and the 1708th at Jeddah, Saudi Arabia. Griffiss crews flew 140 missions and dropped over 2,500 tons of ordnance. The distinctive Statue of Liberty tail markings had to be painted over for security reasons but were repainted following the war.

Col. Michael Drinkhahn (at left), deputy commander of the 416th Bomb Wing and commander of Camp Nacirema, and Lt. Gen. Charles Horner (at right), commander of the Ninth Air Force, make an inspection of Camp Nacirema where a majority of the deployed Griffiss personnel were stationed. In addition to the tanker crews, security police, maintenance, civil engineering, medical, and Rome Air Development Center (RADC) units from Griffiss were present as well. (RHS.)

U.S. central commander and combat commander of Operation Desert Storm, Gen. Norman Schwarzkopf stops for a moment to pose for a picture with two airmen from Griffiss while visiting Camp Nacirema. General Schwarzkopf led the coalition forces that liberated Kuwait in the 1991 campaign. (RHS.)

Over the years the B-52 underwent significant changes and upgrades. The reliable B-52 G model shown above served the 416th well throughout the years. In 1991, the 416th began to receive the B-52 H models. It was equipped with higher efficiency engines, upgraded avionics, and a newly-designed fire control system. The tail defenses changed from four machine guns to a 20-millimeter cannon. (Above, Margo Studios; below, Kevin Kelley.)

Four

SUPPORTING THE MISSION

Upon conversion to an air force base, the duties of the depot still continued to operate eventually under the name Rome Air Material Area, commonly referred to as ROAMA. It was the responsibility of ROAMA to streamline functions and prevent waste or misallocation of resources in the electronics and communications missions at the base. ROAMA was phased out in 1967. (Margo Studios.)

Visitors to Griffiss are given a brief orientation of the facilities at ROAMA and the functions that are carried out in the supply and services directorate. (RHS.)

In 1962, ROAMA was chosen to develop an automated warehousing service that was to be the pilot program for all air material areas in the air force. The goal was to improve the efficiency, inspection, storage, and shipment of electronic and communications-related items. (RHS.)

The Ground Electronics Engineering Installation Agency (GEEIA) was a brainchild of ROAMA. The mission of GEEIA was to take inventions from the design and research phases and make them a reality by engineering and installing communications equipment throughout the world. GEEIA took over the host mission of Griffiss in 1968. (RHS.)

Locally the 2861st GEEIA Squadron was responsible for the installation and maintenance of all communications equipment, including the telephone lines.

Some of the office support at GEEIA gathers around the 10th anniversary cake to celebrate the occasion. GEEIA was eventually absorbed into the Air Force Communications Command in 1970.

The 485th GEEIA was one of the units deployed to set up ground communications in Vietnam and Southeast Asia. Several other GEEIA units served in country, all of which reported to the headquarters at Griffiss. After the phaseout of GEEIA, the 485th was redesignated an engineering installation squadron and transferred to Griffiss, replacing the 2861st GEEIA Squadron. It remained at Griffiss until its deactivation in 1995. (RHS.)

An enduring organization at Griffiss is the RADC. The mission of the RADC is simple: improve on the electronic technology of the day. Radar systems, computer equipment, the invention of the compact disc, the Ballistic Missile Early Warning System (BMEWS), Distant Early Warning (DEW) Line, photonics, frozen lightning, and Pave Mover/Joint STARS were all developed in Rome along with hundreds of other equally important projects. (RHS.)

The RADC played an important role in the space race of the 1960s. On August 1, 1960, NASA launched the first communications satellite, named *Echo 1*. It was a 135-foot inflatable balloon satellite. Once in orbit, a voice signal was beamed from the RADC site at Trinidad, bounced off of *Echo 1*, and relayed back to the Floyd radar site.

A flight test division also operated out of RADC. The flight test division had over 24 aircraft all modified for special testing missions from radar penetration to nuclear cloud sampling. Shown here is a B-45 Tornado assigned to RADC for testing in 1955.

Another unique aspect of RADC was the "upside down air force" testing facility at the Newberg test site. An assortment of aircraft was mounted throughout the years while engineers did all types of experiments on the aircraft. Many upgrades and enhancements were the result of RADC testing. RADC operated 16 offsite testing facilities, each with a specific designated function. (RHS.)

RADC's Electromagnetics Environmental Effects Facility tests the effects that electromagnetic microwaves have on various aircraft electronic systems. (RHS.)

The 4713th Radar Evaluation and Electronic Countermeasures Flight located at Griffiss was an early participant in the development of the Airborne Early Warning System. B-29s were modified with special radar and countermeasure equipment. This B-29, *Necessary Evil*, participated in the atomic bomb attack on Hiroshima during World War II. (RHS.)

Brig. Gen. Alfred Maxwell, the commander of ROAMA, reviews the members of the 4713th during his retirement ceremony in 1957.

Maj. Gen. Stuart Wright (left), commander of RADC, wishes Brig. Gen. Alfred Maxwell best wishes at his retirement dinner in May 1957. Maxwell was awarded a Legion of Merit for years of dedicated service to the air force.

The 2856th Air Base Wing was the military branch in charge of the operational depot functions. When the SAC took over the base in 1970, the 2856th was replaced by the 416th Combat Support Group, which all subordinate military units of the base reported to.

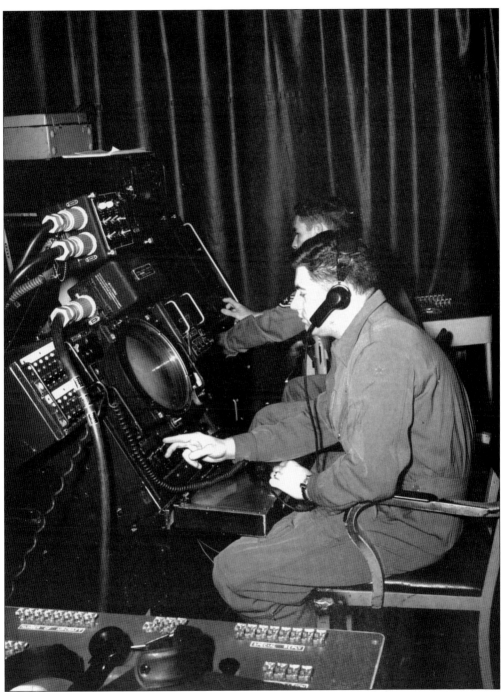

Air traffic control fell under the jurisdiction of the 2019th Communications Squadron. In addition to the control tower duties, it also manned the base telephone switchboard, the telecommunications center, a range of base radio systems, approach radar, the Military Affiliate Radio System (MARS), and other support functions. This small unit composed of military and civilian employees was entrusted with some of the most important support missions on the base. (RHS.)

The 416th Organizational Maintenance Squadron made sure all base aircraft were constantly combat ready. And the 416th Field Maintenance Squadron provided field-level maintenance for base aircraft. The 416th Avionics Maintenance Squadron was responsible for keeping all the base's aircraft avionics systems working properly. Weapons and ordnance were maintained by the 416th Munitions Maintenance Squadron. (RHS.)

RODEO AWARDS - 1953
BASE MOTOR POOL WITH MISS NY STATE

Members of the base motor pool are given safety awards in 1953. To honor this special occasion, Miss New York State was on hand to present the awards. (RHS.)

Griffiss was located near the New York Central rail line, which ran through Rome. A special spur was constructed that allowed locomotives to deliver supplies to the outskirts of the base that would then be ferried to the supply buildings using air force locomotives and rail equipment. (Kevin Kelley.)

The air force maintained two diesel locomotives at Griffiss, as seen in this photograph with the engineers proudly posing in front of them. Special rail lines built during World War II allowed supplies to be brought right to the loading docks. (Kevin Kelley.)

Members of the 416th Transportation Squadron pose on one of the base locomotives. The transportation squadron had the responsibility of transporting troops, cargo, and supplies. (RHS.)

Fire protection services fell under the control of the 416th Civil Engineering Squadron. To say the beginnings of the fire department were humble is an understatement, as many of the early firemen recall only having a plastic helmet, canvas jackets, and fire equipment that was always in need of repair if it made it to the fire.

Major upgrades to the fire department occurred when the SAC came to Griffiss. It was at that time they received new top-of-the-line apparatuses and protective gear. They had a firehouse built to protect the fire trucks from the elements, and it even had a bathroom in it, a necessity lacking from the previous building. (Kevin Kelley.)

The Griffiss Fire Department was segregated into two specifically trained units, structure protection and aircraft crash-rescue operations. It was not until the 1970s that firefighters were trained in both specialties. Unlike many civilian counterparts of the day, the department did consist of both men and women. It also operated the only hazardous materials response team in Oneida County. (RHS.)

Fire quickly spread through the two-story wood-framed ROAMA headquarters building in the early morning hours of January 28, 1961. Fire crews battled the cold weather and intense flames throughout the night; however, the structure was completely lost by daybreak. The only other major structure fire at Griffiss was on March 12, 1952, when the officers mess hall burned, resulting in the death of the officer in charge. (RHS.)

Crash trucks were stationed right on the flight line. Responding to an airplane crash was much different than responding to a structure fire. Spilled jet fuels could quickly ignite and turn into a blazing inferno. Foam was used to extinguish those fires. The local fighter pilots keep them busy. (RHS.)

Accidents happen, and Griffiss firefighters will confirm that fact after responding to a number of downed aircraft over the years. A popular one was the F-94, which by design was a problematic aircraft. Once a pilot laid down his aircraft he was forever subject to the jocularity of his fellow pilots. On a sad note, several pilots did lose their lives at Griffiss. (RHS.)

The crew of this 27th FIS F-94 escaped serious injury, surviving this crash on March 7, 1957, by crashing it into a grassy area of the base. Judging by the nose of the aircraft, which has separated from the rest of the airplane, it hit hard when it came down. (RHS.)

This F-94, also of the 27th FIS, seems to have suffered from some type of onboard engine fire. The blown-off canopy lays behind the F-94, and the remnants of foam on the aircraft and runway can be seen. (RHS.)

Here an F-102 of the 27th FIS sits covered in foam on the runway after an engine fire caused the aircraft to crash on November 26, 1956. A crash-rescue truck can be seen in the foreground. (RHS.)

Word of a KC-135 "flying gas can" fire was not one of comfort to firefighters, knowing that they were carrying 83,000 pounds of jet fuel aboard. When they burned, they burned completely, as shown here. All that remains of this tanker from the 41st AREFS is the wings. (RHS.)

The original base hospital was only designed to be used for 10 years. It became quickly outdated, as it was poorly laid out in design and not capable of supporting the needs of those that needed care at Griffiss. It was replaced with an ultra-modern 70-bed facility complete with an emergency room, surgical rooms, radiology, laboratories, a nursery, and a dental clinic. It even offered veterinary services for families that had pets on base. (RHS.)

Unique gourmet military food items like chipped corn beef on toast or powdered eggs could always be found in the mess hall. Griffiss offered a fine selection of dining opportunities, such as the open mess hall, the officers mess hall, and the social clubs on base, which even served food during the evening hours. Meals were served around the clock buffet style with the hungry airmen choosing what they were going to dine on. Of course one could always wander into Rome to sample the local Italian fare.

Another popular stop for the enlisted personnel was the Mohawk Club, which was located just inside of the Floyd Avenue gate. A wives club also shared the same building, and occasionally they hosted fashion shows, family picnics, and luncheons. (RHS.)

Building 326 housed the Army Air Force Exchange Service's country store. One could find the basic necessities of life in there, such as milk, bread, snacks, and beverages. (RHS.)

The 416th Civil Engineering Squadron Power Production Building was one of several used by the Civil Engineering Squadron. Those not assigned to fire protection were placed on construction-related duties. (RHS.)

Building 428 shared several tenant units. It was the home of the judge advocate and the office of legal services. Several offices of the family services could be found there. And those with a flair for home improvement could borrow tools from the U-Fix-It Shop. (RHS.)

The base commissary was located in building 22. The commissary is the military version of a civilian supermarket. This one was even complete with a deli and bakery. (RHS.)

The base library had an admirable selection of reading materials. In the 1950s, the library received a donation of 1,500 books from the personal library of Lt. Col. Townsend Griffiss. (Kevin Kelley.)

Dedicated reporters and photographers at Griffiss keep readers well informed of the happenings on base. The first base newspaper, the *Vox Prop*, appeared in 1942. During the Griffiss years, readers could peruse the *WAVE Guide*, which then became the *GEEIA News*, and finally ended its days as the *Mohawk Flyer*. The *Mohawk Flyer* was the longest-running series of all the base newspapers. It even won the coveted Top Dog Award in 1974 as the best newspaper in the Second Air Force. (RHS.)

The original 1942 chapel was replaced by a new base chapel in 1970. The new chapel could seat 550 people, and in addition to Catholic and Protestant services there were ministers from Lutheran, Assembly of God, and United Church of Christ denominations. The new chapel also housed offices, classrooms, a library, and meeting rooms. (Margo Studios.)

Wives of the airmen stationed at Griffiss would volunteer their time at the family services center. They were there to help incoming families with moving problems; after all, who would know better than someone who went through it to. (RHS.)

Mrs Kiker puts on FS insignia as Lt Col Wakeman, Mrs Hayes, and Mrs Queen looks on 1963.

Children were frequent guests at Griffiss. Over the years numerous Boy Scout camporees and Explorer programs took place on base with visitors from all over the world. Every year National Kid's Day was also celebrated with the help of the Kiwanis Club. Children and adults alike were amazed at the royal treatment they received on base. (RHS.)

Many of those stationed at Griffiss had families. The children were educated locally in Rome schools and even participated in local sporting events. The Griffiss Air Force Base Little League team is marching in a parade in Rome. (Kevin Kelley.)

No official band was assigned to Griffiss, but it was not uncommon for bands to be requested from other installations to come in and perform for promotions, retirements, and visiting dignitaries. Sometimes it was just for entertainment, as shown here as the Eighth Air Force band delights a crowd in the officers club. (RHS.)

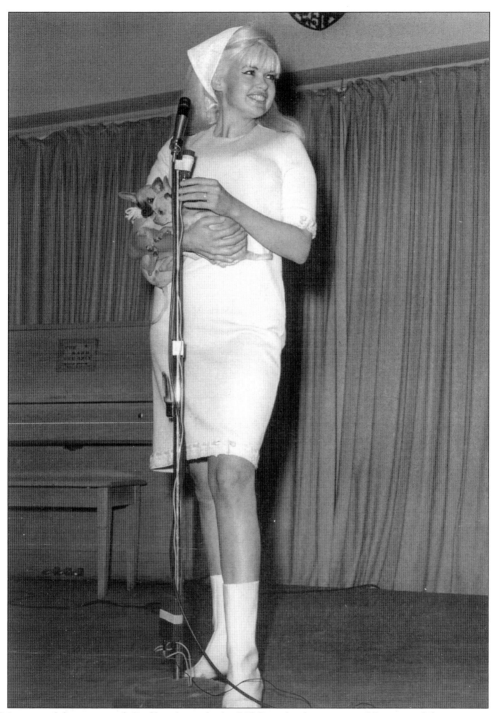

Many a celebrity visited Griffiss through the USO and other venues. Not one of these visits is more remembered or talked about than that of Jayne Mansfield in the 1960s. The model and film star was considered a sex symbol of the era and had many admirers, Griffiss was no exception. Sports stars would even make their way up to the base while traveling through the area. The most legendary was a brief stopover by New York Yankee Joe DiMaggio.

Griffiss was located minutes away from Delta Lake State Park and rivers that provided a better opportunity for fishing rather than the parking lots on base. The scenic beauty of Upstate New York is a year-round attribute that has much to offer for those seeking outdoor activities like hiking and camping. Located in driving distance are the Adirondack Mountains, the 1000 Islands at Alexandria Bay, Niagara Falls, the Finger Lakes, Lake Ontario, and the St. Lawrence Seaway, not to mention New York City, Albany, Rochester, or Buffalo. (RHS.)

For the most part the base was off limits to the average civilian of Rome. However, each year on Commander's Day the base would be open to the public and it would draw large crowds. Often visiting aerial demonstration teams would dazzle the spectators with precision flying maneuvers. A crowd favorite was always the U.S. Air Force Thunderbirds. Shown above is the 1970 demonstration team at Griffiss.

Other demonstration teams included the Navy Blue Angels and the Italian Frecce Tri-Colori in 1987, shown here spraying red, white, and green smoke. (RHS.)

Griffiss was jokingly referred to as the city within a city and had all the modern conveniences of life. However, Rome also had much to offer, and the downtown area was a popular spot to visit on the weekends with the American Corner, the Capitol Theatre, Goldberg's, Candyland, or any number of other businesses and nightclubs.

It was customary for units at the base to lend the community a helping hand whenever possible. Shown are members of the 416th Civil Engineering Squadron assisting John DeProspero, center, with the construction of a bocce court in preparation of the World Series of Bocce. Many alumni of Griffiss became "Italianized" when they visited the city of Rome, enjoying the plentiful Italian food, wine, and hospitality it had to offer.

When the war in Vietnam started to escalate in 1963, so did its unpopularity. The turbulent times of the 1960s and 1970s both at home and abroad combined with the draft reached a boiling point many times. Several local colleges are in the immediate Rome area, which made Griffiss a popular place to expound a message of protest. Large demonstrations of students and clergy were common during the late 1960s and 1970s. The majority of antiwar demonstrations were not violent. The message was a simple one, as shown on the banner.

A large group of Rome policemen stand at the ready in riot gear and armed with batons outside the entrance at Griffiss. They were the first and only line of defense outside the gates of the base.

It was the mission of the 416th Security Police Squadron to defend the base in the event of a breach, and it was never a wise decision to disobey the command of an air policeman. On November 24, 1983, a group of protestors dubbed the Plowshares Seven breached base security and attacked a B-52 and smeared it with red paint to protest the nuclear cruise missiles. The situation was quickly resolved by the 416th Security Police Squadron. (RHS.)

To celebrate the 35th anniversary of the air force in 1982, a number of Congressional Medal of Honor recipients were invited to Griffiss. It was named Project Odin. Odin was the mythological Norse god of war. A handful of recipients did make their way to Griffiss for the celebration, and they included Forrest Vosler, Jay Zeamer, Edward Michael, and Geroge Day. (RHS.)

C-130 HERCULES AT GRIFFISS AFB
ROME, NEW YORK

An assortment of aircraft could have been seen at Griffiss over the years. Shown here is a C-130 Hercules cargo jet. The C-130 is mainly used to transport up to 90 troops, evacuate the wounded, and carry military cargo. It can be modified into heavily armed gun ships or used in search-and-rescue missions. (Margo Studios.)

F-15 EAGLE AT GRIFFISS AIR FORCE BASE
ROME, NEW YORK

The F-15 Eagle was a common sight in the early 1990s at Griffiss. Many of the National Guard units under the jurisdiction of NEADS flew the F-15 while patrolling the eastern seaboard. The F-15 was part of a new series of supersonic, highly maneuverable jets to enter the U.S. Air Force inventory. (Margo Studios.)

Sac's B-1B Supersonic Bomber
Griffiss Air Force Base

This B-1B Lancer makes a pit stop at Griffiss. The B-1 was the last of the sweeping wing design of aircraft on active duty. Traveling at speeds up to Mach 1.25, it has a range of almost 6,000 miles. A variety on munitions may be carried by the B-1. (Margo Studios.)

One of the most important aircraft in the air force is the E-3 Sentry, commonly referred to as AWACS (Airborne Warning and Control System). Through the use of a rotating radar dome, the E-3 provides surveillance, command and control capabilities, and communications to support military missions. (RHS.)

Stealth technology is the wave of the future, and leading that future was the development of the F-117 Nighthawk. Operational since 1987, it was combat tested during Operation Desert Storm. Romans got to view an F-117 at the 1992 Commander's Day. Note the air police maintaining a large perimeter around the aircraft. (Marilynn Kelley via Kevin Kelley.)

The Canadian Air Force also patrolled the skies along the New York border, and to this day it still maintains a regional operational assignment at NEADS. This Canadian CF-100 Canuk was photographed at Griffiss in the 1960s. Pilots also nicknamed it the "beast" due to its sluggish and hard-to-maneuver controls.

The harsh reality of budget cuts hit home hard when Romans woke up to banner newspaper headlines that read "416th Gone!" It was announced on March 13, 1993, that Griffiss would be stripped of all flying missions and subsequently deactivated by recommendation of the Base Realignment and Closure Committee (BRACC). The future of Rome Laboratory and NEADS were also unknown at the time. Almost immediately, the citizens of Rome rallied around with patriotic fervor to protest the BRACC decision. Signs like the one above could be seen everywhere throughout Rome.

BRACC commissioners decided to tour Griffiss after the insistence of the community and local politicians. When the commissioners arrived on May 7, 1993, the local community was out in force waving flags and banners lining Black River Boulevard from Fort Stanwix all the way to Griffiss; they were escorted by wave after wave of Oneida County volunteer fire trucks, marching bands, and roller-blading flag carriers. Impressive as the sight was, it was not enough to reverse the decision of the committee.

On September 22, 1995, after 53 years of service, the 416th Bombardment Wing was deactivated and Griffiss shortly thereafter. All that remains of the air force mission today is the air force research laboratory (a reorganization of Rome Laboratory) and the NEADS. (Kevin Kelley.)

Area politicians lobbied hard to bring jobs into Rome, which had an estimated loss of 5,000 jobs from the closing. The Defense Finance Accounting Service (DFAS) set up operations in the old Supply Depot Building 1 in 1995. The mission of DFAS has been consistently evolving since its formation in 1991, but they provide direct financial support to all branches of the military, including civilians and retirees. In 2005, AFRL and DFAS both appeared on the new BRACC list and survived. As a result of hard work and excellent customer service, a net of 700 new jobs were added to DFAS Rome, making them one of the largest employers in the area with over 1,000 workers. (Tristan Cooper.)

Looking for a location to host the 30th anniversary concert of Woodstock in 1999, the event promoters immediately fell in love with the Griffiss site, which Rome was eager to promote. Word quickly spread of the July 23–25, 1999, concert planned in Rome. The layout was to consist of a stage at each end of the runway and all varieties of venues and vendors in between.When the hoards of music fans began to arrive, it was no wonder why this site was chosen over all others. It was estimated that over 200,000 people visited the concert during that three-day period.

Many men, women, and children came through the gates of Griffiss. Some moved on to other assignments, while others remained in the Rome area to build a new life. Each veteran or civilian employee has their own stories and fond memories of their time at Griffiss. It is those veterans that have made the telling of this history possible. This was Griffiss Air Force Base in Rome, New York. (Kevin Kelley.)

ACROSS AMERICA, PEOPLE ARE DISCOVERING SOMETHING WONDERFUL. *THEIR HERITAGE.*

Arcadia Publishing is the leading local history publisher in the United States. With more than 3,000 titles in print and hundreds of new titles released every year, Arcadia has extensive specialized experience chronicling the history of communities and celebrating America's hidden stories, bringing to life the people, places, and events from the past. To discover the history of other communities across the nation, please visit:

www.arcadiapublishing.com

Customized search tools allow you to find regional history books about the town where you grew up, the cities where your friends and family live, the town where your parents met, or even that retirement spot you've been dreaming about.